# I want to be a Cowboy

## Other titles in this series:

# I WANT TO BE A
# Cowboy

FIREFLY BOOKS

# A FIREFLY BOOK

Published by Firefly Books Ltd. 1999

Sixth printing, 2016

**Library of Congress Cataloging-in-Publication Data is available.**

**Canadian Cataloguing in Publication Data**

Main entry under title:
I want to be a cowboy

ISBN-13: 978-1-55209-447-1 (bound)
ISBN-10: 1-55209-447-2 (bound)
ISBN-13: 978-1-55209-432-7 (pbk.)
ISBN-10: 1-55209-432-4 (pbk.)
1. Cowboys – Juvenile literature.
F596.125   1999   j636.2'01   C99-930933-1

Published in Canada by
Firefly Books Ltd.
50 Staples Avenue, Unit 1
Richmond Hill, Ontario L4B 0A7

Published in the United States by
Firefly Books (U.S.) Inc.
P.O. Box 1338, Ellicott Station
Buffalo, New York, USA 14205

**Photo Credits**

© AISPIX by Image Source/Shutterstock.com, pages 5, 6, front cover

© Jeanne Provost/Shutterstock.com, pages 7, 10-11, back cover

© PD Loyd/Shutterstock.com, page 8

© Kobby Dagan/Shutterstock.com, page 9

© Randy Miramontez/Shutterstock.com, page 12

© Vanessa Nel/Shutterstock.com, page 13

© islavicek/Shutterstock.com, page 14

© Sergei Bachlakov/Shutterstock.com, page 15

© spirit of america/Shutterstock.com, pages 16-17

© Lou Oates/Shutterstock.com, page 18

© JP Chretien/Shutterstock.com, page 19

© iofoto/Shutterstock.com, pages 20, 23

© CandyBox Images/Shutterstock.com, page 21

© Lee O'Dell/Shutterstock.com, page 22

© Laura Gangi Pond/Shutterstock.com, page 24

Design by Interrobang Graphic Design Inc.
Printed and bound in China

Canada ▪ We acknowledge the financial support of the Government of Canada.

Cowboys learn from family and friends. No matter how old or young, cowboys take their work seriously.

Cowboys and cowgirls must look after their horses and equipment.

It takes a lot of practice to be a good cowboy.

One of the cowboy's chief jobs is to round up cows. On a "roundup," cowboys gather stray animals and bring them to one place.

Cowboys make sure their horses enjoy a cool drink after a dusty ride.

Just like the old west, cowboys like to ride together. And every cowboy needs to know how to use a rope.

A cowboy must know how to saddle a horse and make sure everything fits properly.

Cowboys know how to handle their horse in shows where they have to work with stubborn animals like this "ornery" calf.

Some horses are more lively than others. Cowboys need strength and skill.

Some cowboys and cowgirls become rodeo stars. They compete in bronco-riding contests and show off other skills.

Everyone enjoys the roping contest. The rider and his horse know they have to work together.

Cowboys wear heavy clothes for comfort and protection.

A cowboy shoes his horse. He must work carefully to make sure he does not hurt the horse.

Tossing or "pitching" hay is part of the long day's work for this cowboy.

The cowboy's rope is also called a lariat or a lasso. It is used to catch cows or horses. Some lariats are 60 feet long.

Cowboy boots protect the legs and feet. The metal spurs are carefully used to make a horse move quickly.

Riding is great fun, even in the winter snow.

This cowboy is cooking a meal after a long day in the saddle.